THE GIRL WHO COULDN'T TALK DIRTY

THE GIRL WHO COULDN'T TALK DIRTY

Poems

ELISE PANEHAL

© 2018 Elise M Panehal
All rights reserved.

ISBN: 1977511295
ISBN 13: 9781977511294
Library of Congress Control Number: TXU001720362

For Tara, Eva, Keenan and Ryan

CONTENTS

When I Hear Musical Words · 1
Lightning Strike · 3
Bubble Gum · 4
Artist Blind Date · 6
Dare · 7
A Duckling's Secret · 8
Mimosa · 9
Salmon Run · 10
Be a Little Bolder · 11
The Girl Who Couldn't Talk Dirty · · · · · · · · · · · · · · · · · · · 12
Buttercup · 13

The Children Are Coming! · 15
To Tara, Upon Her Arrival to the World · · · · · · · · · · · · · · · 16
Myrtle Beach · 18
Munchkins in Chittenango · 19
Nightlight · 20
Dream On · 22
Butterflies · 23
Good Morning! · 24
China Turkey · 25

Hunting for Reasons · 26
The Children's Hour II · 27
Round the Mulberry · 28
Blessed are the Pie-Makers· 30
One More Ride ·31
Rooster's Rise · 32

Leaving Rome, Moving Home · 35
Moving Down the Canal · 36
Secret Sodas and Muses· 39
There Was a Child Went Forth · 40
Not So Blue Birds · 43
Rats at Five O'clock· 44
Teenagers · 46
Beatles' Business Card ·47
Juggling · 48

Stormy Weather, Lash Me to the Mast· · · · · · · · · · · · · · · ·51
Mayday · 52
Kaleidoscope· 53
Alien Abduction · 54
Dervish · 56
Volcanic Bath· 57
Guillotine Day for Clawfoot· 58
Holy Cards· 60

Lost and Found · 63
Mining · 64
Rip Van Winkle · 65
Francine – Shakespeare Lover· 66

The Doctor · 67
Alzheimer's Ave Maria · 68
Songbird · 69
Comfort Cruise · 70
Zero Man – The Night Writer · 71

Kindred Souls · 73
Move Over Rumi · 74
Brahms · 76
The Brownings' Lovers Leap · 77
Penelope Pining · 78
Lunatic Fringe · 79
Beauty Secrets · 80
Look Out Beach · 81
Yoga · 82
Electric Girl · 83
About The Last Minute Charge · 84
Burning Radiant · 85

About The Author · 87

Moving Forward

For me, poetry is a form of music. It gives words the chance to sing. And I love to sing. Probably because of that, I hear music inside of words. Languages are melodic, too. There's a lyrical juice inside that we can tap and taste. The words we speak have been handed down to us after traveling like tumbleweeds through many countries. Those gypsy words dance off our tongue in a catchy song or a rhythmic poem. This is our language as it centrifuges down to us today.

My thanks go out to:

My children Tara, Eva, Keenan and Ryan. When they were little, we read poems by candlelight between ice cream sundaes while four-foot snow drifts graced our doors in Rome, New York. We kept the beat with drums and tambourines. Special thanks to Tara for her beautiful book cover design and lovely poems. And to Eva, thanks for the fine-tuning edits and charming limerick and poems.

My mother Francine. She was a writer and a poet and loved Shakespeare. Her poem is included in this collection.

My father Bob. He regaled us with his stories and puns over dinner. He was also a medical man, who doctored us, body and soul.

My stepmother Kat. She is my loving fan who encouraged me to finish this book.

My friend and editor Claudia Taller. She persevered through my first draft and the ones after. She is an author and the founder of Word Lovers workshops and retreats.

The muse. She woke me every morning at 4:30 a.m. with the whisper of, *'Get up and write!'*

A fortune cookie. It gave me this message: 'We are here to create, not merely survive.'

Acknowledgments

The poems "Moving Down the Canal," "Hunting for Reasons," "The Children's Hour II," "Alzheimer's Ave Maria," "Francine - Shakespeare Lover," and "To Tara upon Her Arrival to the World" were published by The Rome Observer in the 1990s. Thanks go to its charismatic editor, Carl Eilenberg, the former mayor of Rome, New York. "Nightlight" was printed in the Hessler Street Poetry Anthology in 2008. "Round the Mulberry" was printed in the Cuyahoga County News Notes in 1998. "Rip Van Winkle" was featured in an online anthology by the Cleveland Writers from South Euclid and performed in that town's historic library. "Look Out Beach" was published in the Emerald Necklace Metroparks Magazine in 2014.

Contributing Authors

This collection houses three generations of accomplished female writers. I am humbled and honored to have such designing women as collaborators.

Francine Panehal my mother, attended Baldwin Wallace College and was awarded an Honorary Doctorate by Ursuline College. She was the State Representative for Cleveland, Ohio for 14 years and also served as the State Minority Whip.

Tara McKnight (Shank) my older daughter, graduated from Bowling Green State University, with a BFA in Graphic Design. She is the Art Director for Array Creative in Akron, Ohio and she designed the cover of this book.

Eva McKnight (Schock) my younger daughter, graduated from Denison University with a BA in English and a Master's Degree in Non-Profit Administration. She is a grant writer for the Cleveland Rape Crisis Center.

WHEN I HEAR
MUSICAL WORDS

LIGHTNING STRIKE

So, strike me,
Fell me.
If I move too fast
Through this hum-drumming
Me-me mediocrity,
I'll shuffle then,
Even limp.
Or punch a hole in my roof
So I can see the stars
Again and again.
And I don't mind,
If the birds come perch
In this dumbstruck tree.
I'll just scribble down the songs
They sing to me.

BUBBLE GUM

I know that a lot of
What I stuck in here is
Bubble gum,
Right out of my mouth.
I'm asking you
to chew it with me.
Beautiful or gross,
It doesn't really matter,
Just know that I love you.
Before you put on your sneakers,
better check them.
My gum might be in there.
Your sweet toes
could glue together,
Go amphibian.
Blame it on me,
Just my silly putty.
If I grab it back
it might become
a lucky penny!
With my face stamped on it,
I can launch a thousand ships
With one royal word.
But now a bird,
a robin red breast
Snatches it.
She's patching her nest,

Filling in the chinks
Around her brood.
In a flutter of wings
it falls.
Pick it up,
Dust it off.
Blow me a bubble!
I kissed it.
It's clean.

ARTIST BLIND DATE
Adirondacks, Old Forge, New York

Drive into the blue.
Find the tree that breezes you.
Braille your way along the bark.
You will feel the letters carving,
See your name curling,
In the soundless cerulean sky,
Because
Everything is breathless,
Waiting for you.

DARE

Take the dare,
The dive, the dance step.
Take the guitar off the wall.
Plunker, twang it
Flunker.
Flail.
Be labeled,
Tabled, skewered
Sewered.
Let connoisseurs
Nail you.
Touché,
Bullseye,
Right into the target.
You know it's better,
Far better
Than perfection
The Big Lie,
Paralyzed.
So, go on.
You just might be mediocre,
A happy dilettante,
With a Cheshire smile.
Take it.

A DUCKLING'S SECRET

As the ugly duckling growing up,
The family's fall guy, its comic relief,
I was shocked to hear mom say,
As I trip-danced down the steps in 5th grade,
"My God, you have perfect legs."
I, alien child, looked up startled.
Years flew by.
Now, after my nasty divorce
I do the cha-cha until the wallpaper curls.
And I smile at the surprises
Inside of me.

MIMOSA

My life is
Folding and unfolding the
Burning shade's kisses
into perfume,
Spinning earth and
green woolies into fantasy colors,
Humming, dancing
at the loom.
I'm artless.
Do not pick me.
I don't need pity in a vase
to be pretty.
I'm beautiful.

SALMON RUN
Fish Hatchery, Rome, New York

Salmon run upstream, red scream,
To their river-mother's mouth,
Where they were born.

BE A LITTLE BOLDER

Step it up.
Take the bright path
Singed in sunlight,
Laced with the laughing brook.
Don't falter, don't trip
on the sad stones,
Stewing in their fossils.
So? Let them sing too!
There's room for hummingbirds
And dragonflies,
And boulder beauty.

THE GIRL WHO COULDN'T TALK DIRTY

When he asked me,
Everything zipped up.
I couldn't do it.
I couldn't *talk dirty*.
But the earth kept spinning,
And my crooked smile
Kept grinning.
How could I ask that of my mouth,
When I live to sing?
How could I break my own heart
and pretend to be
Just any 'thing'?

BUTTERCUP

Little one,
Peeking out from behind a crevice,
I know your heart so well.
You are in love with the sun.
He has you at his beck and call.
And if you are beautiful,
Your love makes you so.

I, too am matched with such a son,
Kindled in heaven
Fired on earth.

One look to him,
And I'm dazed,
Burnt to the ground,
But still standing,
Like you.
My soul is colored, only,
With deeper and deeper hues.

THE CHILDREN ARE COMING!

TO TARA, UPON HER ARRIVAL TO THE WORLD

This poem is simple and sober
Its theme is related to hope.
In a world that is fractured and frantic,
And has lost its true vision and scope.

But each time a new child arrives here,
One can't help but grasp at the chance.
Can this be the one who erases,
Sad songs, "It's the very last dance."

One can't help but tender the option,
And hope that their wings are pure gold.
That all of their missions are noble,
And all their intentions strong hold.

Fate plays its very own prologue,
Fate fools and connives with us all.
But fate is a flickering candle,
That sputters and dies at the wall.

And the wall is the world of decisions,
Be they good, be they bright, be they wrong.
And only in doing our utmost
Do we nurture the brave and the strong.

What is strength without testing and sorrow?
What is life without a firm quest?
Are we only the grim reaper's plaything?
Why not shoot for the moon with our best?

We will drink a toast of thanksgiving,
Bless the good, and the bad, and the gone.
We will drink a toast to tomorrow,
Give us courage and heart to go on.

So welcome, our very new member,
To a world with a flickering light.
That flicker must grow to a fire,
Of intentions, both noble and right.

White horses, parades did not greet you.
You came with a sweet little sigh.
We are counting on you for the future.
Pluck those heavenly stars from the sky!

Francine M. Panehal
1/27/86

MYRTLE BEACH
Myrtle Beach, South Carolina

Last night Eva found a jellyfish,
And Keenan caught a crab.
Crawling in our spotlights,
Flooding ocean on our hands.

The beach at night is haunted by
The likes of you and me,
Catching up on constellations
And the peaceful crash of sea.

Am I an oxymoron
To go roving in the night,
Clutching little hands and batteries,
Bags of shells and borrowed sight?

The tide eats Tara's castle
And makes mockery of her moat.
Our little family craves these waves
To keep our hearts afloat.

MUNCHKINS IN CHITTENANGO
Chittenango Falls, New York

"She's really most sincerely dead."
-- The Coroner, from *The Wizard of Oz*
                    (the musical)

A yellow brick road
Ribbons through
Chittenango Falls, New York,
Frank Baum's hometown.
Near its deafening cascades,
He surely found Oz,
And a muse or two.
The townsmen built the golden path,
Brick by brick and
The Munchkins *did* come,
The Coroner, Mayor and Slovak trumpeter,
High-pitched, strutting, wizened,
But very much alive,
Telling stories of mighty midget orchestras.
They sport tuxedoes and grant autographs.
The coroner measures his friends,
For next year's suits, then
"They're off" again!

NIGHTLIGHT

"If it's any constellation to you
There's a star up there for every child on earth
Past, present and future."
He was more talkative than he'd been in a long time,
And it was a stunning night.
"Imagine looking up and seeing no lights,
Just a vacuum..., not good," God says, "Not good.
So I leave the lights on for them."
He winks at me. "Are you connecting the dots here?"
The clichés are killing me.
A neon Motel 6 flashes through my mind.
"You're in good company with the Greeks
and Egyptians," he says,
"Now *they* had a handle on the night skies.
Abraham was equally jazzed with the desert sky,
The promise of children as many as the stars.
And did he ever run with that!
What children, and so talented!
So I leave the toys out at night.
If they can't sleep, the kids take out their #2 pencils,
Connect the diamonds,
Find their favorite animals and
Steer their ships by the bright ones.
They're not alone crawling around in a black hole.
They'll find their way back to me," he says,
"If they do a good star search and
Stop staring at their shoelaces.

I guess it's kinda like that Motel 6."
"You mean 'we'll leave the light on for you'?" I offer.
"Yeah, like that, am I a good parent or what?"

DREAM ON

Dream on about the flowing river
Dream on about the sparkling stream.
Fly with the running deer forever,
But don't shed a tear
'Cause I'll be there, I'll be near.

Dream of the running ponies,
Running with the wind.
Dream of the eagles flying your way
Dream of the ocean so blue
A whale comes out just to see you.
You feel light as a cloud, you do.

Climb up to the highest mountain top.
Dive into the deepest sea.
Take a breath of fresh air
And you'll never wake from your sleep.

Tara McKnight (Shank) Age 10

BUTTERFLIES

Butterflies fill my eyes
With flutterings and flaps.
Lead me to the river
And across the lake.
I will always follow and
I will always wait,
Right behind you.

Eva McKnight (Schock) Age 9

GOOD MORNING!

The sunrise is a fiery red
And brings the wondrous morning.
But you don't wish to get out of bed,
It came without a warning.

You were awake all night you say
And didn't sleep a wink.
Well, it's the start of brand new day.
Give it some thought, THINK!

Although you don't want to go to school,
And it's much nicer just to lay.
Sleeping in, is still not cool,
Because…..SURPRISE! It's Saturday!

Eva McKnight (Schock) Age 9

CHINA TURKEY

There once was a turkey from China,
Who loved to eat out at a diner.
Each time he ate out,
The people would pout,
And he would go home looking finer.

Eva McKnight (Schock) Age 11

HUNTING FOR REASONS

I wandered down the path with you,
Mind-melted with the snow.
But you pulled the trigger on the poem
When you dragged home the doe.
My toddler needs me to explain
Why little Bambi is in pain.
Ego systems, that *wild* taste,
A caveman needs some food.
Can't you find a better way
To keep yourself amused?

THE CHILDREN'S HOUR II

On the day the clock spun back,
One sparkling hour slipped out,
Unmeasured, unsifted,
As the first snow fell.
And my children,
Raced into it,
Faces to flakes,
Packing, rolling out,
A family of snowmen!

ROUND THE MULBERRY
W. 116th St. & Lake Ave., Cleveland, Ohio

Cracking the wall
In 'the heart of it all,'
Is a mulberry tree,
Next to the Christian Science Church,
History's octagon,
Which none can call back
To its pulsating jewel life,
Like that of the black-and-blue
Spattering the concrete
Mulberry tree.

Clutching at fireflies,
Keenan, the drummer boy,
Swallows it all with his eyes.
He beats his bodhran, bags empty,
Berries stain the goatskin.

Eva, the dancing girl,
Flashlights up the branches,
Purple lips in the dark,
Bobbing berries in her hair,
Blue-blood on our sticky fingers,
Mulling over this very moment,
Pulses pounding.
There will be cobbler tonight.

<u>Our</u> mulberry tree!
In the heart of this city,
We own you,
Because we love you,
Breaking through the church wall,
Sweetly sweating
Mulberries.

BLESSED ARE THE PIE-MAKERS

Woods Wanderer,
Trees sprouted in your mind.
My children cradled
in the lush boughs
Of your plantings,
Apple seeds.

Lugging bags,
Bigger than they.
Life had its sad, sour times.
Our answer was always the same.
"Go out to the porch,
Grab me some apples,
We'll bake apple pies."
Each one waves a mini-rolling pin.
Pounding that dough,
With a big "A" cut in,
Our lives came bubbling up,
Under a perfect crust.

In memory of Ohio's Johnny "Appleseed" Chapman

ONE MORE RIDE
Rome, New York

Home is where the heart's left.
Dogs bark,
I open the mailbox
Grab the last paper,
A friend's final wave
And we move on.

But up the road
The swaying corn
Whispers.

Memories flood to Old Forge,
Water roller coasters spiral in my mind.
They hurl me back to the mountains
And never unwind.
It's my family's enchantment.
Our first slides, first boats, first bikes,
Tumbling into the roaring waters.
Farewell.

Now here, in this dirty teeming place,
I thought I saw a familiar face.
"Just one more ride on the roller coaster,
Mister?
Just one more ride!"

ROOSTER'S RISE
The Cumberland Gap, Kentucky

Rooster tickles the sun
With a feather under her nose,
From her place of repose
In the Cumberland Gap.

And now,
To wake the mothers.
He has the soulful strut down,
The mourning music
Crowing high with a bumpy
Screech,
Ending in a tri-tone trail off,
(Just so they know how hard he works).

The world may be clockless
But it cannot go cockless..
And, a cackling voice reminds him,
The job has its perks,
Pulling the hens
Out of their dream sleep,
Their preening-precious REM
Again and again.
God knows
He does it for chickenfeed.

Up and down,
Up and down,
This feathering and
Fathering.

LEAVING ROME, MOVING HOME

MOVING DOWN THE CANAL
Rome, New York

Water roads and other modes of
Transport came to town.
Therapyland took hammer in hand
To pound Rome's plaza down.

In search of where America began,
A quivering pen in Bellamy's hand,
Allegiance to a flag unfurled,
Faith in a never-ending world.

Buildings blistery, crying history
Fell, Fort Stanwix rose.
Soldiers haunt the sentry posts,
Flies taunt an old mule's nose.

Young Gansevoort refused to bend,
And led his loyal desperate men.
To turn the tide of raging war,
Defiantly they cut the cord.

Starved patriots at Valley Forge
Found friendship's corn in outstretched hands.
Through seven hundred snowy miles,
Trekked Polly Cooper and the Oneidans.

From across the sea Von Steuben came,
That Baron of old Prussian fame.
He brought our rabble to decorum,
Taught them to march in proper form.

Passed the baton, these precious men,
An army to George Washington.
The Baron chose to call his home
A two-room cabin close to Rome.

A long velvety look from Sal,
Dare I forget Erie Canal,
Rome's opening in 1825,
The waterway that changed our lives?

The waves of corn rustle the wind
Awash with smells of succotash,
And apples full up to the brim,
Between the sheaves three sisters dance.

Oh Running Deer, to have no fear
And live in deeds that nobly stand,
To put the hands and feet on dreams
Sings in the marrow of a man.

Now planes will come and planes will go,
The Erie does move rather slow.
Sal swats at one more fly and brays,
'The naysayers will not have their day.'

One of a kind they take their place,
A soldier's step, a dancer's grace,
Oliver's anxious cry for 'more,'
Sue's set the stage and knows the score.

Matthew smiles at crowded aisles,
The Capitol breathes again!
Maxwell's silver songs beguile,
Lifting the hearts of friends.

A love-worn shawl, a hand-sewn flag,
The city's tailor mends its dream.
And history will never know
Where is the tear or hidden seam.

Let us mosey down the Erie.
Let the water nap our dreams.
Just go down a piece to Granny's.
Lap your name along the streams.

Across our cheeks, the racing tears,
Fireworks burst and slice the night.
With the babes in love we bore here,
Our packet boat moves out of sight.

SECRET SODAS AND MUSES

4:26 a.m.
Half asleep, I hear the
Suction, separating sound
Of the fridge door opening.
My son is sneaking a soda,
'Soda' in New York,
Where he was born,
'Pop' in Ohio, where we live.
He does this many nights.

4:27 a.m.
Something is shaking me awake
(the muse grabs me by the hair)
Tells me "get up and write!"
She does this in the sliver of time
When dawn cracks open the day.
Is each minute of life a
Cameo shoot?
In this frame –
I share this secret time
With my son.

THERE WAS A CHILD WENT FORTH
Rome, New York

There was a child went forth every day,
And the first object she looked upon, that object she became.
And that object became part of her for the day,
Or a certain part of the day,
Or for many years or stretching cycles of years.

The billowing branches of the maple trees,
Friends on summer days became part of this child.
And the velvety irises, faint scent of tulips, the soft peony buds,
And the rickety wooden fence with the red peeling paint,
And the green, sticky butternuts from the neighbor's tree,
And the chatter of squirrels arguing over the day's meal,
All became part of her.

The children taking their precious pennies to buy candy
At the corner store became a part of her.
And Mrs. Esposito bringing chocolate chip cookies to the new neighbors,
And the laughing boy playing baseball in the street and racing on bicycles,
And the Gantniers coming over to play their weekly scrabble game,
All became part of her.

Her own family, her parents became part of this child.
The mother always humming or singing a song,
The comforting words, the kiss goodnight,
The father's calm presence, piggyback rides
And strong arms bent around her,
The younger sister's innocent blue eyes, sucking her thumb,
The blanky worn from love trailing behind,
The two giggling brothers' round rosy cheeks,
All became part of this child.

The whitewashed church and playground down the street,
All became part of this child.
And the railroad tracks that a train never crossed,
And the Iron Kettle Restaurant,
Where pancakes waited every Sunday,
And the sandy beach along the shore of Delta Lake,
And the Children's Museum with the giant bubble wands,
And Fort Stanwix where the flashing colors of fireworks
Appeared every Fourth of July,
All became part of this child

The quiet streets, the sun disappearing behind the storefronts,
All became part of this child.
The townspeople returning home for dinner,
The day's laundry taken off the lines,
Carefully folded and put away,
Green beans picked off the vines growing up the garden fence,
The world a safe place, tucked into bed with teddy,
A bedtime story 'round the corner,

These became part of that child who went forth every day,
And who now goes, and will always go forth every day.

Tara McKnight 12/13/01   Age 16

NOT SO BLUE BIRDS
RTA Rapid Station, Brook Park, Ohio

Like giant berries
They hang on the prickly bushes
By the train tracks,
Hundreds of blackbirds,

In the early dawn,
Their deafening cacophony
Is all the rage,
As we silently
Trudge up the platform,
Grimacing against the wind.

We can look forward to their
High society chatter
For the rest of the season.
What's the latest?

RATS AT FIVE O'CLOCK
E. 40th St. and Euclid Ave., Cleveland, Ohio

You had a date with fate I'd say
At 40th and Euclid last Monday,
Hoisted upon your own petard,
A whiplashed rat, squashed in the yard.

You parked your carcass in plain view,
Flattened like a playing card.
I called the city's clean-up crew,
But all they did was disregard.

Ten days of trudging o'er your spot
We rue the day what God hath rot,
And wish your smudge would wash away.
Yes, even a rat must have his day.

Vicariously we live our lives,
Vermin in each other's eyes.
Paws, think upon their simpler fare.
Their vittles? Vaguely we're aware.

Jaw-opened cans and pigeon stew,
No more to feast upon the trash.
No more to play king of the hill,
Queen for a day, jack of the swill.

Each day we dance around your mess,
Spiffed up we are in business dress.
But each breath, still, comes from the Word,
And not a single one's absurd.

TEENAGERS

At the drop-off
He took my last dollar.
I let this happen
Over and over.
I'm just a doormat
With arms clutching
A steering wheel.

I drive to work on
Financial fumes,
Hearing the pennies
Slugging it out in the
Bottom of my
Purse.

BEATLES' BUSINESS CARD

I tossed out all but one
Of our dumb business cards.
But it came in handy
When McCartney blew in.
I knew I'd meet him,
Aching for his autograph
On Tara's kids' book,
Ricky Joins a Band,
With the Rickenbacker,
His smiling guitar she drew.
Instead he signed
Our old Celtic card,
Remnant of an Irish duo,
The Fab Two,
Immortalized by a Beatle's hand.
I'll never wash it,
Yeah, yeah, yeah.

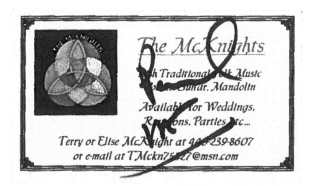

JUGGLING

You juggle the balls of
Happy and sad and
Utter a prayer.
They hover in the air.

If you clap you won't catch
the rounds of applause
In the claws
Of the audience
You can't see.

How will this circle ever be
More than heart songs
And soul whispers?

Etched in the sky
Are the smoky colors
Of a rainbow,
God's half-smile.
Illumined in the windows
Are figures of bards and saints,
Heroes once, but now?
They're just shards
of shattered glass,
Caught in the act
And struggling.

Oh idle hands,
Formed in a
Lover's workshop.
Let's do some juggling.

STORMY WEATHER, LASH ME TO THE MAST

MAYDAY

The first of May, my birthday
You dropped the mini-bomb.
We were going bare-bones,
Exchanging token gifts.
Mine was a perfunctory
Bottle of perfume and a raggedy
"I don't give a shit" bouquet.
That was 1990.
It should have been a
Wake up call,
But for the kids and
Me so blind.
It took another ten years
For me to get it,
That it really was
Mayday,
And this ship
Was going
Down.

KALEIDOSCOPE

No it's not frightening,
It's just me
Stuck in my patterns.
Stars cascade and scatter,
As I collide and cope
With crashing worlds.
The colors churn
As my inner tube
Turns.

ALIEN ABDUCTION

A lien on my house!
The bank has me in their sights now.
I walk out the revolving door,
Squinting at the Canada geese
Squawking overhead.
The flying saucers
Cloak themselves
In the
Flock.
Floating pink lights
Peek through
Gray-green feathers.
The next thing I remember
Was
Staring
at an oval table
In a whirling disco.
As we entered French airspace,
My frog-faced abductor
Flagged down the waitress
For the tab, "le billet,"
Cursing her in
Sum-spitting
Dialect.
Then,
His finger
Hovered

Over a pulsating
Pink button on an
Out-of-control panel…
And,
For what it's worth,
That's the last I saw
Of Mother
Earth.

DERVISH

My atoms are
Nano-tornadoes,
A whirling dervish of
Energy swirling,
Swooping up particles,
To suggest a shape.
My destiny,
What is it?
Dusty me,
In frequency.

VOLCANIC BATH

The bathroom floor is
Erupting.
Planks are rising.
Water is on the move
Between the grooves and
I'm walking on a volcano.

Our clawfoot tub could
Crash down to the basement
Anytime now.
Ten years in this house and
It feels like a Century Home,
Screaming to be rebuilt
Room by room.
I pry open the bathroom door and
Finally call my cousin, Don,
The plumber,
"She's gonna blow!"

GUILLOTINE DAY FOR CLAWFOOT

Strains of the *Marseillaise*
Could be heard
Marching through the
Family's throats.
It was guillotine day
For the porcelain tub.
The Empress' hand had fallen.
Clawfoot's efforts to bribe her
With a little *gateau* had failed.
She'd stopped eating cake.

I read him his last riot act,
Channeling up all the Renoir
I could muster,
To paint his final fleeting face,
With the trickle tears.
Attends! A reprieve,
A trapdoor rescue,
But *non, simplement*
A sledgehammer,

UPS'ed in from Paris.
I avert my eyes,
Hearing his lost wet whisper,
"Je vous en prie!
Allons enfants de la Patrie."

HOLY CARDS

Pick a card, any card.
So I picked Joan of Arc
Floating on a
Lavender cloud.
She jumps down
from the church window.
Confirmation queen, I am,
Singing Catholic songs
So sweetly!

But it was never enough,
Guilt flows like a river.
Charismatic, now
I morph into a zealot,
Neatly "arranged" to be an ideal family.

The things I didn't know.
With four babes in tow,
I'm married to a man whose
Shining armor is empty.
Clankety clank,
He ran away.

Now, alpha and omega am I
To these four little souls.
Sure wish I had
A real hand to hold,
Instead of these holy cards.

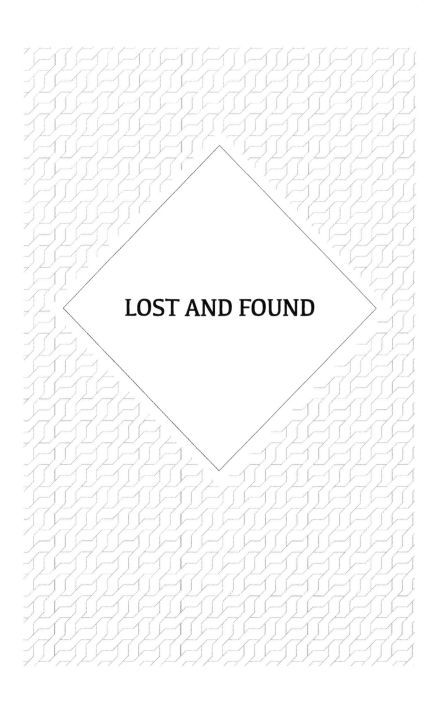

LOST AND FOUND

MINING

Tear your Madonna eyes from the sky.
Grab a hard hat.

Tears of exhaustion stream and
The collection basket rolls by, empty.
There's nothing left to give.
Now I'm a mother to a family
Where the loveless man walks away.
And I saved the world?

But now look, you see?
There's a collapse in the mine.
And you gotta go down there,
'Cause one of those bodies in the rubble
Is you.

So tear your Madonna eyes from the sky.
Get your hard hat, for God's sake.
Go save yourself.

RIP VAN WINKLE

Beauty wakes to a peck on the cheek
From a crow
Her knight in shining ardor
Split.
She's been sleeping for 25 years?

Mirror, mirror,
Her kingdom for a mirror.
The children have grown,
Oh let them sleep a little longer.

She trucks into town and
A few people greet her
With a "where the hell have you been?"
The local coffee shop fills her up
With the day-to-day.
They take her pulse
And she takes theirs.

She cries to think of all she's missed.
Really lets it
Rip.
Then, picks up her crown
And her train,
And choo-choos out to
Check on the royal crew.
She's back.

FRANCINE – SHAKESPEARE LOVER
For my Mother

You walk along sonnet-filled halls.
Queens carry your train,
Asking for counsel and advice,
Your "wise saws and modern instances."
Fancy that, Francine,
Your stage.

It's true, I've seen you there.
The grace of your mind
Fills your heart, your voice,
Your feet.
When frailty finds you
Your spirit is elsewhere,
Supping at high tables
Blessed with your presence.

The small, the great,
All love you,
Hoping you will sit by them.
Fancy that, Francine.
Fancy you.

THE DOCTOR

The doctor delights in the children,
Enchanted ones.
He cherishes every flutter of life
The earth brings forth,
Knowing in a heartbeat,
That birth is a miracle.
And once in a lifetime
Could happen forever.
He also finds the time,
Infinitely, patiently,
To cradle the ancient children, too,
Still in their enchantment,
Blessing the soil with their beloved forms,
And the heavens,
With their quickening souls.
A healer, his hands shine with spirit,
All ready.

ALZHEIMER'S AVE MARIA

Francine's outer faculties
Don't know you.
But her spirit may,
If the treasure door
Chooses to open today.
She could say something
Coherent.
Otherwise, she's a
Ball of emotions.
Like a baby,
She hears your heart.
Never assume she isn't
Grasping inane conversations.

She sang the *Ave Maria* with me
On the day before she passed.
Mom, you were still there.

SONGBIRD

The cardinal kisses the wind,
its voice, sweeter for the sorrow.
A missing mate,
the nest,
the wait.

COMFORT CRUISE
To Bob and Kat Panehal

They were sad to the second power,
Widow and widower, ages 81 and 79,
Nurse to her man for 10, and to her mom for 5,
Caregiver to his wife for 15,
Vowing to be in his own dirt bed
Within the year.

Both sent on a comfort cruise,
Just in time for a Kodak moment,
'C'mon get in the picture lovebirds!'
And two strangers' eyes meet
For the first time.
Does she know how to eat *escargots*?
She gives him a Boston accent "no."
He shows her how, she's radiant,
Her blue eyes beaming.
They dance the night away
And live happily ever after.
I'll tell this true fairy tale
Forever.

ZERO MAN – THE NIGHT WRITER

He feels like a zero
As he burns his words into the night.
His angry hot writing,
Scratches at featureless faces,
That fail to embrace even the thought
Of how much they were loved.
He pours out the lava language
Onto some unsuspecting paper Cinderella,
And watches it turn into a fireball.
Remembering who he is,
He sings around the embers,
Laughing at the life in his veins.

KINDRED SOULS

MOVE OVER RUMI

Rumi whispers,
"Don't go back to sleep."
So I'm up at 4:00 a.m.,
Talking to ghosts of Christmas past,
Talking trash, talking zero.
I feel the empty pockets,
Some no jobs, some slow money,
No room at the inn.
Rumi, it's a sin to be poor
on Christmas,
Oh yeah.
I'm feeling the "o" in snow,
So cold, we gotta dig down deep
Underneath the pennies.
I'm talking deep, below
In the plexus with the butterflies,
Where songs and love run wild.
And a child can be born again,
Where bikes turn into planes,
And the senile talk sense.
Words are pure songs.
Down there, I feel the lining in my pockets.
And Rumi still won't let me sleep,
Not until I touch the inside
Of his magic hat, again.
Yes, I nod, it's really empty.
And then I touch it.

The nothing is electric.
In the middle of the zero,
The cup is brimming over,
Full of love, and only love.
Finally, I feel it.

Move over Rumi,
I'm just talking in my sleep.

BRAHMS

Brothel serenades
Were the tunes you played
When the Schumanns found you.

Lullabies for their babies,
Diaper duties late into the night,
What didn't you do for love?

There is a bittersweet
Crossing of beauty and pain
In your symphonies.
Dear to Robert,
Dearer to Clara,
Johannes.

THE BROWNINGS' LOVERS LEAP

So brave.
You took your love,
Eloping from the 'hood,
that suffocating *Rule Britannia*.
Elizabeth, an invalid,
Clings to Robert,
A clutch of poems in her pocket,
Leaping as one
Into a Florentine painting,
Italy!

PENELOPE PINING

She offers me a thumbnail sketch.
"My life," she says, "is not the stuff of legends.
It's not idyllic, waiting for Ulysses."
Her voice drifts off.
She interviews three more suitors,
Would-be wooers,
A young knucklehead,
Who wears his nothingness well,
A lawyer with his lawsuit and
Big plans for the kingdom,
And a politician,
Who will take the burden of female rule
Off of her 'still pretty' little shoulders.
Dodging their advances,
Penelope weaves into the night.
She scans the horizon, crying,
"Ulysses will return."
They're eternal lovers,
Not bound by this earth.
She meets me for coffee the next morning,
Puffy-eyed, with a quivering smile.
She glances out to the Aegean.

LUNATIC FRINGE

I love wearing dresses
Trimmed with fringe,
The way it shimmers
In the moonlight,
When I dance to Sergio Mendes,
Or Earth Wind and Fire.
The fringe might be
Medusa's extra curls
On a boy or a girl,
Pulling the
Suzy-perfect features
A little askew,
To subtly infer
That bigger dynamos
Whirr this universe,
Than the tight little ways
We package ourselves.
Every creator has
A little madness
In his ear.
The moon pulls the ocean,
Making the fringe
Sway.

BEAUTY SECRETS

If my socks don't match.
Try not to stare.
No pancake batter on my face,
And I do not dye my hair.
When it's gray, I'll embrace my tendrils.
"A woman should never tell her *real age*."
I told people that I was a year older
For a *whole year*.
I actually could not remember,
Nor act, my age.
When my birthday came,
It was a Big Surprise!
No Sew Unisex Advice:
Holes in your jacket pockets can be
Stapled closed with a red desk stapler.
The pennies like to tunnel around
In your jacket lining, so they'll be
Crying in their copper cups.
But they'll get over it.
Final tip:
You know you are beautiful and
No make-up can ever hide that.
So, why bother?

LOOK OUT BEACH
Edgewater Park on Lake Erie, Cleveland, Ohio

The sunset worshippers are coming,
With their dancing-to-the-drums feet,
Stomping to the Beatles revival.
Surfers hoist their paddleboards.
Doggies wag behind their yoga masters.
See how they toe your deserted sands.
You're all combed out and raking in the crowds!
This ruckus, the stampede, what's it all about?
As if the lake was just discovered.
The sand didn't suddenly wake up!
For heaven's sake, you've been here all along - years.
Fingers point every which way,
But put one on the pulse and get it,
Because it's us resuscitating,
Us, clamoring for life,
Cleveland, a whole city,
Sitting on a beach, singing.
So, look out beach,
Cameras are running,
Look alive!

YOGA

Yoga poses
Tender questions.
Muscles wince as
I breathe and move
Through my planks and dogs,
Corpse and sphinx.
I resurrect,
Relax and exhale,
Bowing over a suppler
Bended knee.
Giving a little more to the pose,
My humble warrior
Answers.

ELECTRIC GIRL

I'm a lightning rod.
The words speed through me.
This surge of poetry is
Pulling me out to sea.
Tell me I'll finish this last one
Before I'm electrocuted.

ABOUT THE LAST MINUTE CHARGE

As the Pied Piper of this Enterprise
I must tell you that the door to
Book Mountain was closing.
Most of us were already inside
When Electric Girl came hobbling up.
She wasn't on crutches,
But she might as well have been.
The tears were real, and her combo
Of saltwater + electricity was
Making the other poems nervous.
She could short circuit permanently!
Time for an editorial decision.
So Electric Girl wants in, I muse.
We sure could use her extra energy,
And I don't think I've ever heard her *talk dirty*.
Where there's a will, there's a woman.
Book Mountain turns emerald green..
"Dry those eyes E-girl, we've got the go-light.
Play the last notes on your penny whistle Ryan."
The door to Book Mountain closes.
Tiny blue flowers cover the cave door's cracks.
No one will ever find us.

BURNING RADIANT

My dreams are
My spirit children,
With a fire in each one
Burning radiant.
I am feeding them.
They are beginning
to run now.
In time,
They will feed me.

ABOUT THE AUTHOR

Elise has been writing poetry since eighth grade when she was asked to memorize and recite "All the World's a Stage." It was love, and no stage fright.

She was born in Cleveland, Ohio and studied at Northwestern University. Her desire to become fluent in languages took her to Europe, where she lived and worked in Germany for three years. In 2009, she graduated from Baldwin Wallace College with a Bachelor of Arts degree.

Elise raised her four children in Rome, New York. She moved back to Ohio to care for her parents and currently lives in Berea, Ohio.

Her poems have appeared in the *The Rome Observer*, the *Emerald Necklace Metroparks Magazine*, the *Cuyahoga County News Notes* and in the *Hessler Street Poetry Anthology*. This is her first poetry collection.

In addition to writing, she has performed Irish traditional music at the Irish Cultural Festival in Berea and at many schools and libraries. She is a soloist in area churches and has recorded two Irish traditional CDs as well as a jazz sampler.

Elise is well over 40 but well under 100. She's never been one to act her age.

Elise Panehal
elise.panehal@gmail.com